This book belongs to ....

of the ....Six in the ....

..............................Cub Scout Pack

Home Address ....

....

Akela's Address ....

....

Sixer's Address ....

....

Group Scout Leader's Address ....

....

So you have joined the Cub Scouts! Welcome to the world-wide Brotherhood of Scouts.

There are over fifteen million Cub Scouts, Scouts, Venture Scouts and Leaders all over the world! So you have joined a very large Movement!

You'll have lots of fun and you will be able to take part in many new activities . . .

The first thing you are going to do is to gain your Cub Scout Badge. This will help you to get to know what Cub Scouting is all about.

Then, at a special Investiture Ceremony, you will make your Promise and become a member of the Scout Movement.

The Cub Scout Badge

You become a Cub Scout when you are invested. Being invested means that you make your Promise to Akela, in front of the Pack. It is an important ceremony, because when making your Promise you become a real Cub Scout and a member of the world-wide Brotherhood of Scouts.

Before this happens, though, you will have to gain your Cub Scout Badge which will help you to find out all about Cub Scouting.

Here are the things you have to do:

1. Be told the first Jungle Story and how Cub Scouting began.

2. Know the Grand Howl.

3. Know the Scout salute and sign, handshake and motto.

4. Know the Cub Scout Promise and Law.

The Jungle Story

Do you recognise these names? They are the names by which the Pack call their Leaders. Do you know why? The first Jungle Story will tell you.

Akela will tell you this and other stories from *The Jungle Book,* then you will know who all the characters are.

Chil
Akela
Bagheera
Mowgli
Raksha

How Cub Scouting Began

Lord Baden-Powell was a brave and famous soldier who travelled the world. He taught his troops to follow tracks, to travel across country without being seen or getting lost and to look after themselves whilst camping out. He called these soldiers 'scouts'.

When Lord Baden-Powell returned to England he wrote all that he had taught his soldiers in a book called *Scouting for Boys*. So many boys wanted to do the things they had read about that B.-P. (as he was called) left the army to devote more of his time to the new 'Boy Scouts'.

The sort of Scouting B.-P. wrote about was meant for bigger boys of over eleven, but because all their younger brothers kept joining in the fun, B.-P. started the Cub Scouts for them.

All this happened way back in 1916 and hundreds of thousands of boys have enjoyed being in the Cub Scouts ever since.

The Grand Howl

This is a very special greeting that the Pack gives to Akela. It helps the Pack to remember the Promise they have made. When you have made your Promise you will be able to join in.

The Pack forms a circle and Akela stands in the middle. He shows you when to start by lowering his arms. The Pack squats and calls;

'Akela! We'll do our best'.

The Pack jumps up, arms by sides and the Sixer calls;

'Cubs! Do your best'.

And, with a smart salute the Pack calls back;

'We WILL do our best'.

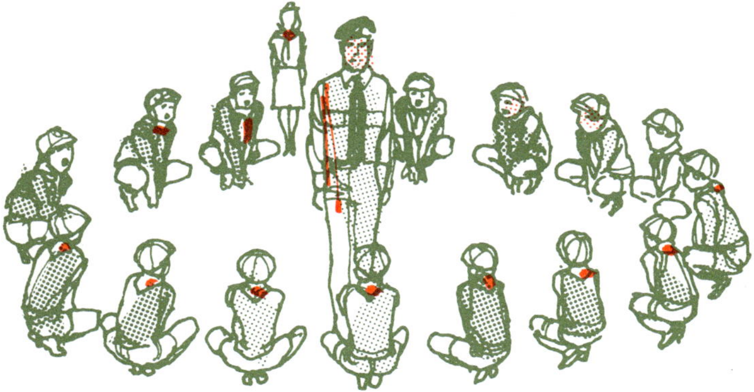

The Scout Salute

All Scouts use the same Salute as a sign of friendship. Use it when you meet Akela or the other Leaders; you will also use it in the Grand Howl and during Flag Break.

The Scout Sign

When you make your Promise you will salute at shoulder-height. This is called the Scout Sign.

The Scout Handshake

In Africa, where spears and shields were used in a war, it was a sign of great trust to offer your left hand when shaking hands. In this way, you had to put down your shield and yet leave the other person with his spear in his hand. All Scouts shake hands left-handed to show their trust in one another.

The Motto

'Be Prepared' is the Scout Motto. Are *you* prepared for anything? You should be, now that you are becoming a Cub Scout.

The Cub Scout Promise

I promise that I will do my best
to do my duty to God and to the Queen,
to help other people
and to keep the Cub Scout Law.

The Cub Scout Law

A Cub Scout always does his best,
thinks of others before himself
and does a good turn every day.

Meet the Chiefs

On page 8 you read how Lord Baden-Powell started Scouting. In 1920 he was proclaimed 'Chief Scout of the World', no-one but B.-P. will ever hold this title. Since his death in 1941, the United Kingdom has had four Chief Scouts.

The Lord Somers KCMG DSO MC

The Lord Somers was born on the Isle of Wight in 1887. He went to Mulgrave Castle and Charterhouse Schools and Oxford University. He served in the Army during the First World War then, in 1926, he was appointed Governor of Victoria,

Lord Somers

Lord Rowallan

Australia and was made State Chief Scout. In 1941 he was elected Chief Scout of the United Kingdom and continued to work very hard for Scouts until his death in 1944.

The Lord Rowallan KT KBE MC TD LLD DL

The Lord Rowallan was born in London in 1895 and he went to school at Eton. When he was 18 he joined the Army and fought in the First World War. After the War he joined the Scout Movement and, during the

Lord Maclean

Sir William Gladstone

next twenty years, he held various positions. He was Chief Scout from 1945 to 1959 and, during this time, he travelled to many countries to visit Scouts.

The Lord Maclean KT KBE

The Lord Maclean was born in London in 1916 and went to Canford School in Dorset. When he was living in London he joined the Wolf Cubs (as Cub Scouts were called then) and has been a Member of The Scout Association ever since. In 1959 he was made Deputy Chief Scout and later that year he became Chief Scout. In 1971, Lord Maclean was chosen by Her Majesty the Queen to be her Lord Chamberlain and so he retired as Chief Scout.

Sir William Gladstone BT DL MA

The present Chief Scout is Sir William Gladstone and he is the great-grandson of the famous Prime Minister W. E. Gladstone. Sir William was born in Buckinghamshire in 1925 and went to school at Eton. He served in the Navy from 1943 to 1946 and then became a schoolteacher – and eventually became Headmaster of Lancing College. Sir William is married and has two sons and one daughter. He was appointed in 1972 and will be retiring in Spring 1982.

The World Badge

When you have made your Promise and become a Cub Scout, Akela will give you this badge. It is called the 'World Badge' because Scouts in countries all over the world wear the same badge.

It shows that young or old, big or small, whatever language we speak, we are all Scouts. So be proud of your badge, you've earned it – and now you are ready to take part in the Arrow Scheme . . .

The Arrow Scheme

There are three Arrows, which you gain in this order, Bronze, Silver, then Gold. You should try to gain all three before you move on to the Scouts.

How do you gain each Arrow Badge?

You will be able to select a number of activities from the lists shown in this booklet. You will need to take part successfully and show progress in each activity.

The activities are divided into four areas:

Growing up	Discovering
Thinking	Sharing

What do you have to do for each Arrow?

FOR THE BRONZE ARROW

Take part in the first activity in each area, then choose two more activities from each list. When you have completed twelve, you'll have the Bronze Arrow.

FOR THE SILVER ARROW

Choose three more *new* activities from each area; when you have completed twelve, you'll have the Silver Arrow.

FOR THE GOLD ARROW

Choose another three *new* activities from each area; when you have completed twelve, you'll have the Gold Arrow.

By the time you've reached 'Gold', you'll have taken part in thirty-six different exciting activities!

How do you choose the activities?

Talk about the Arrows with Akela and together decide which activities to take part in for each one. Choose something new – things you have never done before – they are more fun and there's no point in trying something you can already do, is there?

Marking off your activities

Colour in the feathers of each Arrow on your *Cub Scout Membership Card* when you pass an activity. You will also find these Arrows printed on pages 58, 59 and 60 of this booklet.

Remember, twelve activities make one Arrow.

Good Luck with your Arrow programme – have fun!

Growing up

. . . to be fit and able to take care of yourself

1. Lay a trail of tracking signs and follow a trail laid by someone else.

2. Practise so that you can take part successfully in a game involving ball throwing and catching.

3. Practise any three sports training activities, such as skipping, balancing, somersault, leapfrog, etc.

4. Go for a walk with an older person and explain how to use the *Green Cross Code.*

5. Improve your memory with observation games.

6. Climb up a tree or rope.

7. Make your own bed and find out how to make your bed in camp.

8. Cook a simple meal indoors.

9. Learn to swim. Discuss the water safety rules with other Cub Scouts or a Leader.

10. Ride a bicycle safely.

11. Pack your kit after playing football or going swimming, or unpack and put away your kit after returning from a holiday.

12. Know how to apply simple first aid and how and when to get adult help.

13. Play in a team for at least four matches.

14. Go on an expedition of at least five kilometres with a Scout or an adult.

15. Take part in an emergency drill and know what to do in case of a fire.

16. Help to pitch a tent.

17. Explain to a Leader how to keep yourself fit and the dangers of damaging your health.

18. Use a compass to find your way to a secret destination.

19. Swim 100 metres. Discuss the water safety rules with other Cub Scouts or a Leader.

20. Go on an obstacle course, including such things as a monkey bridge, rope swing, climbing net, etc.

21. Make a first aid kit and know how to use the contents. Take it with you on an outing.

22. Light a fire out-of-doors and cook something on it.

23. With a grown-up try a new sport, such as roller-skating, ski-ing, judo, fishing, horse riding, sailing, canoeing, trampolining, etc.

24. Help to build a tree house.

25. Learn how to tie your tie and your shoelaces.

Discovering
. . . new skills and interests

1. Use two of the following in an activity: reef knot, clove hitch, round turn and two half hitches, bowline, highwayman's hitch, hank a short rope.

2. Find out about the three crosses of the Union Flag and learn the National Anthem. Know what to do when flags are flown and national anthems played.

3. Make something from odds and ends.

4. Find out something new about any animal, tree, fish, bird or plant which you see on an expedition.

5. Discover something of interest about the Royal Family, such as types of transport they use, their hobbies, places they visit, etc.

6. Grow a plant in a garden or a plant pot.

7. Draw or paint a picture of any subject of your choice.

8. Think up and use a secret code.
9. Take care of a pet for at least a week.
10. Make and fly a kite.
11. Make a puppet and take part in a puppet play.
12. Provide the birds with food and water regularly.
13. Watch three different types of machinery at work, such as a crane, caterpillar-tracked vehicle, combine harvester, earth mover, tractor, fishing boat gear, etc. Explain to a Leader the work they do.
14. Play at least three tunes on a recorder, guitar or other instrument.
15. Find out something about exploration, for example in space, underwater or underground.
16. Make something out of wood, metal or other material using the correct tools.
17. Help an adult with the routine maintenance of a bicycle or other

machinery like a model railway, sewing machine or a car.

18. Carry out three scientific experiments.

19. Make up a story of about 100 words and tell it to your Pack.

20. Collect five foreign coins. Explain how much they are worth and explain the symbols on them.

21. Construct a working model such as a drawbridge, a conveyor belt, a windmill, etc.

22. Make a plaster cast of an animal's or bird's footprint. Discuss its way of life with other Cub Scouts or a Leader.

23. Find out more about Baden-Powell and how Scouting began.

24. Find out the emblems of three airlines and the types of aircraft they use. Explain why airlines use the 24-hour clock.

Thinking

. . . about ourselves and others

1. Keep a diary of good turns for a week, showing how you have helped other people.

2. Draw, act or tell the story of someone whose job it is to 'help other people'.

3. Offer to do two good turns at home – and do them.

4. Visit an old people's home, children's home or hospital ward and help to do something useful, as a Pack or Six.

5. Make a 'Thank You' card or write a letter and send it to someone on behalf of the Pack.

6. Find out about someone who has 'done their best' in the past. Act or mime the story.

7. Explain some of the country's laws about litter, why these laws are made and how you can help to keep them.
8. Assist at a Service at your own place of worship.
9. Look at five different advertisements on television or in magazines and explain which you think does the best job.
10. Take part in a Pack Meeting about Cub Scouts in another country – the games they play, their activities, their language and food.
11. Help a newcomer to settle in at your school or Pack.
12. Write some prayers for use by your Pack.
13. Find out something about life in your area in the past and act any special events or describe any interesting buildings.

14. Explain to a Leader the meaning or reason for different Services in your Church, Chapel or wherever you worship.
15. Learn to speak five useful phrases in another language.
16. Carry out a survey of boys' clothes, find out what your friends think about them and what they like wearing best.
17. Make a poster to advertise Cub Scouting to younger boys.
18. Find out something about three different forms of communication, such as radio, television, semaphore, smoke signals, drums, newspapers, telephone, etc.
19. Keep an account of how you have spent your pocket-money for a fortnight, showing what you have spent on sweets, clothes, presents or other things, and how much you have saved.
20. Help to plan and carry out a conservation project.
21. Help to organise and take part in an act of worship for the Pack.
22. Invite a nurse, doctor, fireman, clergyman, policeman or social worker to your Pack Meeting to talk about their work. Then discuss with your friends how you could help them.
23. Find out something about two forms of worship which are different from your own.
24. Help to welcome visitors to your Pack Meeting and make them feel at home.

Sharing

. . . our thoughts and experiences with others

1. By acting a playlet with your Six or with a friend, show how accidents in the home can be prevented.

2. Find out the meaning of the badges which were given to you, when you were invested. Fold your scarf properly and find out why you wear it.

3. Draw five traffic signs or symbols and know what they mean.

4. With a friend, make use of two of the following – an adventure playground, a library, museum, art gallery, leisure centre, swimming pool or supermarket.

5. Use a public telephone and a private telephone.

6. Invent a 'car passenger code' of behaviour and some travel games.

7. Go on a Pack Holiday spending at least a night away from home.

8. Walk round your local area following a sketch map; mark on it the position of your home and other important places such as your school, Church, Pack meeting place, park,

shops, garage, bus stop, telephone kiosk, etc.

9. Arrange to invite a friend or two to your home for a meal which you have helped to plan, cook and serve. Clear up afterwards.

10. On a Pack outdoor activity show that you know the *Country Code* and the reasons for it.

11. Visit a railway or bus station and learn how to use a timetable.

12. Help your family to plan and go on an expedition. Tell a Leader about it afterwards.

13. Offer to do three different jobs for a person such as a farmer, postman, policeman, forester, fisherman, road-man, district nurse, etc., and do them. Tell the Pack about it.

14. Show a friend around a place of interest.

15. Make a chart of all the people who help to run your school, showing the different kinds of work they do. List the ways you can help your school.

16. Go on an expedition to a place such as a fire station, farm, news-paper printing works, telephone exchange, rubbish disposal plant, a radio station, television centre, lifeboat station, etc. Discuss how they help the community with other Cub Scouts or a Leader.

17. Using a map, help to plan a route for your summer holiday or a Pack expedition.

18. Go on a Cub Camp, spending at least a night under canvas.

19. Make your own weather station with at least two instruments. Keep a log over a period of a fortnight (charts, comments, drawings, etc.).

20. Describe to a Leader three different television programmes you have seen in a week.

21. Help the Pack Leaders to plan and run an outing.

22. Help another Cub Scout to do something he finds difficult.

23. Take part in a play, concert or Group show.

LITTER

Proficiency Badges

While you are working on your Arrow Programme, you can also earn lots of badges. Look at the list on your *Cub Scout Membership Card* and decide which ones you'd like to try. The requirements are all on the next few pages. You can start as soon as you are invested.

COLLECTIVE ACHIEVEMENT BADGES

You will notice that some of the badges are marked as 'Collective'. This means that they can only be taken by a group of boys who work together, so that they can all gain the badge. This group could be your Pack or Six – or even you and some of your friends from various Sixes in the Pack.

THREE STAGE BADGES

The Swimmer and Athlete badges have three stages. When you have passed Stage 1 you wear a badge with a red background, when you pass Stage 2 you add a badge with a yellow background and when you pass Stage 3 you add a badge with a green background, so you have either one, two or three badges according to how many stages you have passed.

Animal Lover

Choose any two of the following alternatives:

1. Keep a scrapbook and tell the examiner about any six animals you have seen (not native ones), their countries of origin, feeding habits and details of the special care they need.

2. Look after a pet for at least three months. Keep a record of its feeding habits and how you have looked after it. Know how to recognise common illnesses and what special care is needed before and after the birth of young animals.

3. Help to care for a farm animal for a season. Keep a record of its feeding habits and the kind of work you have done. Know how to recognise common illnesses and what special care is needed before and after the birth of young farm animals.

4. Belong to an animal or bird society. *Either* take part in one of its activities *or* make progress in any award scheme offered.

5. Keep a record (e.g. in pictures, sketches, photographs or on tape), for one month of bird, animal and/or insect life in your garden or specific area in a park or farm.

6. Find out about one of the following: bird life; butterflies, moths or other insects; native wild animals; friends and enemies of the garden; seashore, pond or river life.

Artist

Choose any three of the following alternatives, at least one of which is to be done in the presence of the examiner:

1. Draw with a pencil, brush, pen or crayon an original illustration of any incident, character or scene, size not less than 18 × 13cm (7 × 5 inches).

2. Design and make a greetings card.

3. Make a model in clay or other plastic material. Size not less than 10 cm (4 inches) square.

4. Make a decorative article from cane, raffia, wool, leather, wood or any other suitable material approved in advance by the examiner.

5. Make a design and print it on paper or fabric (e.g. using potato cuts or lino cuts).

6. Make a worthwhile toy or model of a reasonable size.

7. Undertake a project, having agreed it with the examiner, involving the use of a plastic or metal construction kit. The standard expected should demand an imaginative approach and a high quality of workmanship.

Athlete

A THREE STAGE BADGE

You must gain the following points from four previously chosen events: 22 points for Stage 1; 30 points for Stage 2; 35 points for Stage 3.

1. 50 metres Sprint

10 points	*7 points*	*5 points*
9 seconds	10 seconds	11 seconds

2. Throwing the Cricket Ball – using 135 gm (4¾ oz) ball

10 points	*7 points*	*5 points*
30 metres (100′)	24 metres (80′)	18 metres (60′)

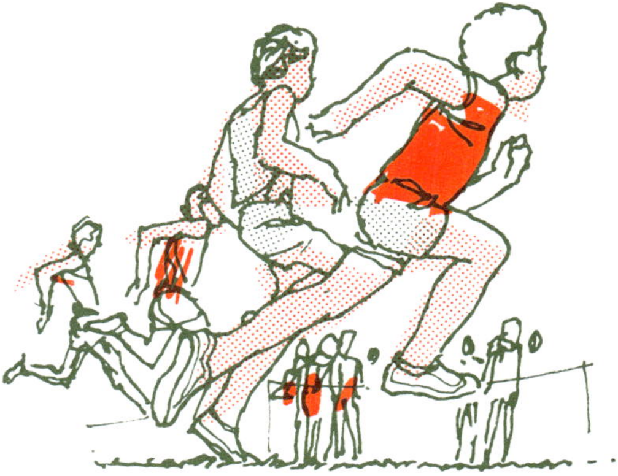

3. High Jump

10 points	*7 points*	*5 points*
0.96 metres	0.86 metres	0.76 metres
(3′ 2″)	(2′ 10″)	(2′ 6″)

4. Long Jump

10 points	*7 points*	*5 points*
3 metres	2.5 metres	2 metres
(10′)	(8′)	(6′ 6″)

5. 400 Metre Run

10 points	*7 points*	*5 points*
90 seconds	100 seconds	110 seconds

6. Sargent Jump – measurements refer to height on target

10 points	*7 points*	*5 points*
35 cm	30 cm	25 cm
(14″)	(12″)	(10″)

Note: When Requirement 3 is undertaken, special regard must be given to the nature of the jump and the landing facilities required. Unless expert tuition and supervision is available the Fosbury Flop should **not** *be attempted.*

Book Reader

1. Produce a list of books you have read recently, name their authors and be able to tell the examiner something about three of the books. The three books to be chosen by you are to include at least one story and at least one factual book.

Note: The three books must be of a reasonable standard, taking the Cub Scout's age and development into account.

2. Show that you understand how to care for books.

3. Show that you can use a dictionary, encyclopaedia and an atlas.

4. Explain to the examiner how the books in a library are set out and how you would find a specific fiction book.

Camper
(Collective)

Carry out the following as a member of a group of boys and not by yourself. This group could be your Pack or Six.

1. Camp overnight under canvas on two separate occasions.

2. Pack your own kit for a weekend camp.

3. Help to pitch and strike a tent.

4. Know how to care for a tent at camp.

5. Make a simple camp gadget.

6. At camp help to prepare, cook, serve and clear away a simple meal.

7. Know the basic health and safety rules for camp.

8. Help to tidy up the camp site before you leave.

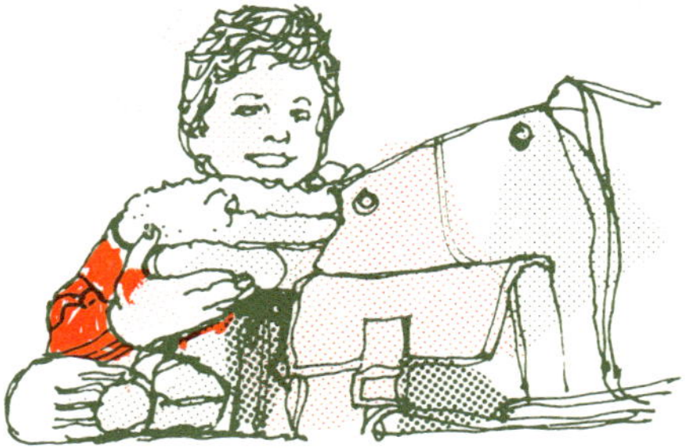

Collector

1. Make a collection of a number of similar items (e.g. stamps, postcards, matchboxes or fossils).
2. Arrange your collection neatly and systematically, labelling items correctly and clearly.
3. Talk about items in your collection that particularly interest you.
4. Visit a collection made by someone else and explain what you like or dislike about the presentation of the collection, choice of venue, etc. This could be a personal or public collection.

Communicator

1. Demonstrate how to use the telephone and know how to make an emergency call.

2. Write a formal letter (e.g. thanking a visitor to your Pack).

3. Choose any three of the following alternatives:

(a) Send and receive three short messages using signals (e.g. Morse code, semaphore).

(b) Make a verbal report of a local event either past or present.

(c) Write and decipher three simple messages in code.

(d) Hold a simple conversation in another language.

(e) Make and maintain a link with another Cub Scout Pack through tapes, letters, etc.

(f) Hold a simple conversation without talking (e.g. by manual alphabet or understand and read a piece of Braille writing).

(g) Memorise a message and deliver it twenty minutes later.

Cook

1. Plan, cook, serve and clear away a two course meal for at least two people.
The following dishes are given as suggestions. You may produce your own menu which will be approved by the examiner beforehand.

Main Courses
Shepherds Pie
Egg Salad
Sausage Rolls
Cauliflower Cheese
Fish Pie
Puddings
Baked Apple with custard
Fruit Crumble
Eve's Pudding
Jelly Whip/Trifle
Suet Roly-Poly

2. Know how to prepare and cook fresh vegetables.
3. Make either scones, small cakes, biscuits or tarts.
4. Make and serve a hot drink.
5. Know the basic rules of safety and hygiene in the kitchen and the reasons for them.

Cyclist

1. Own or have the regular use of a bicycle of proper size.
2. Be able to mount and dismount properly.
3. Be able to clean and oil a bicycle and pump up the tyres.
4. Understand the need for keeping the bicycle in a road-worthy condition, and help to do this.
5. Understand the need for keeping a bicycle locked when leaving it unattended.
6. Know how, and help, to mend a puncture.
7. Under observation go for a short ride on a specified course, showing a knowledge of the proper use of those signals and rules applicable to cyclists as set out in the *Highway Code* in the section for the Road User on Wheels and Extra Rules for Cyclists. (The route shall, if possible, include a cross-roads, pedestrian crossing, right-hand turn and roundabout.)
Note: A Cub Scout who has passed the National Cycling Proficiency Test of the Royal Society for the Prevention of Accidents qualifies automatically for parts 2, 3 and 4 of this badge. The National Cycling Proficiency Test will only qualify for part 7 if it included a test on the highway.

Entertainer (Collective)

Carry out two of the following as a member of a group of boys and not by yourself. This group could be your Pack or Six

1. Create a play and perform it.

2. Make puppets for, and produce, a puppet play or shadowgraph.

3. Produce a recorded show (e.g. for someone who is housebound).

4. Sing a programme of songs, carols or hymns.

5. Perform some folk dancing.

6. Make a selection of simple rhythm instruments and use them as an accompaniment to songs.

7. Perform a display of tumbling tricks.

8. Make up and produce short dances to pieces of music of your own choice.

9. Take an active part in a Pack band or Gang Show.

Note: Other forms of entertainment of comparable standard are acceptable if they are agreed with the examiner beforehand.

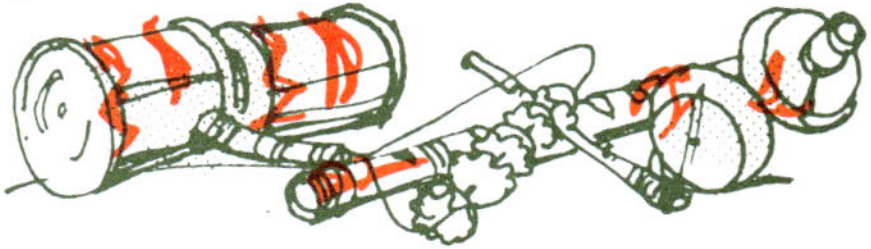

Explorer
(Collective)

Carry out the following as a member of a group of boys and not by yourself. This group could be your Pack or Six.

1. Discuss with the examiner the preparations required for a one day expedition in the countryside, e.g. cost of expedition, correct clothing, footwear, first aid kit and food.

2. Take part in two Cub Scout expeditions, one of which must be entirely out of doors.

3. Build a simple shelter.

4. Build and light a fire outdoors and then make a hot drink.

5. Find your way to a place in town or countryside, 1 kilometre (half a mile) away, by following directions given to you by the examiner (either compass directions or signs made on the ground, or landmarks, or a combination of these).

First Aider

1. Know the limits of first aid and the need for getting adult help.

2. Know how to control bleeding by direct pressure on a wound.
3. Know the importance of cleanliness and show how to dress minor cuts and grazes with gauze and roller bandages; apply and remove adhesive dressings.
4. Demonstrate the use of a triangular bandage as a large arm sling and a knee bandage.
5. Demonstrate how to make a patient comfortable.
6. Know the common causes of burns and scalds in the home and their prevention; how to put out burning clothing; the simple treatment of burns and scalds.
7. Have a knowledge of the mouth-to-mouth method of respiratory resuscitation and where possible demonstrate this method by use of a manikin or approved aid.

Fisherman

1. Hold the Swimmer Badge (Stage 1).
2. Know the dates of the closed seasons and the minimum sizes of fish which may be retained for the areas in which you fish.
3. (a) Know how to remove a hook from a fish's mouth without damaging the fish and how to kill the fish properly.
(b) Recognise six different fish from photographs. Know the best baits to use for any four fish, the places in which they lie and the best way to fish for them.
4. Keep a log book over a period of three months of fishing trips undertaken. The log to contain a note of water conditions, weather, wind direction and strength, species and numbers of fish caught and baits which prove successful.

Gardener

1. *Either* look after a patch of garden for at least three months. Know what tools are needed and how to use and look after them. Grow something in your garden suitable for the time of year. *Or* grow a variety of plants indoors and know the conditions under which they must be kept.

2. Choose any two of the following alternatives:

(a) Grow vegetables or flowers from seed; know how to prick out and transplant.

(b) Know about hazards to plants and flowers (e.g. diseases, pests) and understand what preventative measures can be taken and what can be done to aid growth.

(c) Find out about one of the following: trees and shrubs; wild flowers; friends and enemies of the garden; ferns or grasses or other plant life.

(d) *Either* know how to store vegetables and how long they may be stored, *or* show how to prepare flowers for display to give maximum effect.

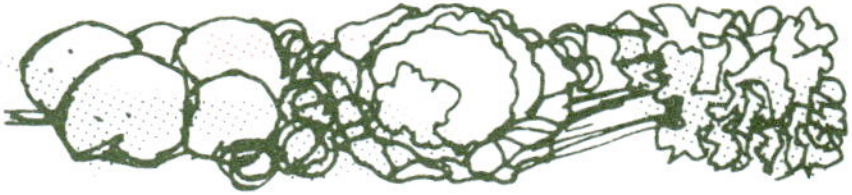

Handyman

1. Know what to do in the event of a burst water pipe or gas leak and know what to do in an electricity power cut and how to turn off the electricity supply at home.
2. Know the colour code of electric plug wiring and demonstrate how to change a plug.
3. Know what to do in the case of fire.
4. Make a useful article for use in the Pack Den or at home.
5. Demonstrate the use of and how to take care of the following tools: hammer, saw, screwdriver, spanner, pliers.
6. Make and put in a suitable position a nesting box or bird table.
7. Demonstrate how to prepare and paint a vertical surface and clean a paint brush.

Hobbies

Show a continuing interest and progress, over a period of at least three months, in a hobby or skill; be able to demonstrate it and/or discuss it with the examiner.

Note: Suitable hobbies might be collecting, chess, singing in a choir, etc. A Cub Scout may gain and wear any number of Hobbies Badges subject to his pursuing each hobby for three months.

Home Help

1. Fry bacon or sausages; boil, fry or poach an egg; prepare and cook potatoes.
2. Lay a table and serve a simple meal. (This can be done in conjunction with 1 above.)
3. Wash up afterwards and show how to deal with a saucepan, cutlery, glassware, etc.
4. Wash and iron your Group scarf.
5. Sew on a badge or button.

6. Make a bed.
7. Clean windows, and silver or brasswork.
8. Clean and tidy a room.

Map Reader

1. Know the principal signs used on a 1:50 000 scale O.S. map of your locality. Be able to pin-point your home and Pack Den. Explain how well-known local features of your choice are represented on the map.
2. Make a scale model of an 80 metres (250 ft) hill – showing the contour layers at regular intervals.
3. Understand all of paras. 1 and 2 so that you can describe what you would see along a 5 kilometre (3-mile) stretch of road set by the examiner on any 1:50 000 scale map.
4. Set a map and know how to use a compass.

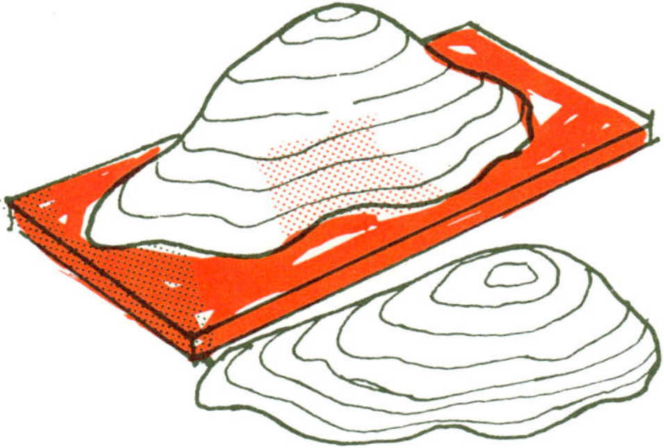

Musician

1. Explain the major symbols on a musical score and give the correct meaning of common musical terms.
2. Sing two songs or play two pieces of your own choice which show different styles and tempos.
3. Choose any two of the following alternatives:
(a) Sight read a simple piece set by the examiner.
(b) Demonstrate some musical exercises which improve your playing or singing.
(c) Name the parts of your instrument or know how your voice works.
(d) Know how to look after your instrument or voice.
(e) Know the storyline of an opera, ballet or folk song.
(f) Clap out the rhythm of a piece played by the examiner.

Photographer

1. Take a set of twelve pictures or 2½ minutes of movie film describing an event or outing. These should be of varied subjects (e.g. landscapes, people and action shots) and may be in colour or black and white, and home or commercially processed. N.B. All twelve pictures or movie film need not necessarily be taken on the one occasion.

2. Discuss with the examiner the main features of a camera (i.e. shutter speeds, lens focusing and apertures) and films. Explain how they are used to ensure technically good results. If you have an 'instant' camera explain how the film is instantly developed and demonstrate how to load the camera.

3. By mounting the prints or projecting the transparencies, use them to describe to other Cub Scouts the outing or event mentioned in paragraph 1.

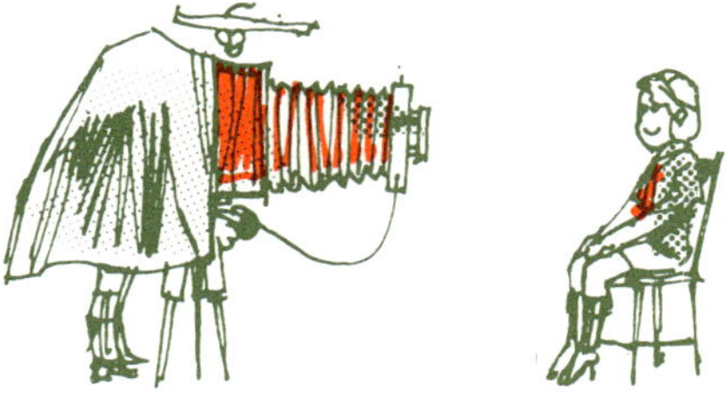

Rescuer

1. Hold the Swimmer Badge (Stage 3).

2. (a) Understand and where possible demonstrate the following methods of rescue – the reach, throw, wade and row.

(b) Enter the water, swim 25 metres to the subject. Tow for 25 metres, using a towing aid, e.g. lifebuoy, piece of wood, etc., and on completion of the tow secure the subject in the support position.

(c) Jump or dive into the water, surface and swim 10 metres. Recover an object 2.5–4.5 kilogrammes (5 to 10 lbs.) from a depth of at least 1.2 metres (4 feet). Bring to the starting point using life-saving backstroke.

(These tests need only be done in swimwear.)

3. Using a training manikin where possible demonstrate the expired air (mouth-to-mouth) method of respiratory resuscitation to the satisfaction of the examiner.

4. Answer four questions on water safety.

5. Show methods of rescue, and the precautions to be taken in the case of ice-breaking and an outbreak of fire indoors.

Note: A Cub Scout who has gained the Elementary Award of the Royal Life Saving Society qualifies automatically for parts 2, 3 and 4.

Scientist

Choose two experiments from each section of the badge and explain to and/or show the examiner what you have done. Where appropriate explain any conclusions you have made.

The Home

1. Connect up simple circuits with bulbs, batteries and switches.

2. Demonstrate that electrical currents produce magnetic, chemical and heating effects.

3. Find out about what happens when you mix lemon juice and baking powder.

4. Make an invisible ink from a household substance.

5. Make some yoghourt and find out how living creatures are involved in the process.

6. Find out how well your house is insulated (e.g. the loft, water pipes, water tank, cavity walls); suggest how the amount of insulation could be increased to advantage.

The Physical World

1. Make an artificial rainbow by splitting up a beam of white light.

2. Make a pin-hole camera.

3. Keep simple weather records over a month (e.g. rainfall, temperature, cloud cover, wind direction).

4. Make a simple periscope.

5. Make a telephone using string to

transmit the sound.

6. Demonstrate how to recover dissolved substances from sea water or river water.

The Living World

1. Grow cress (or similar plant) and investigate what happens when light and water are excluded from it.

2. Use a net and jar to find out how many different creatures live in the water and mud at the edge of a pond.

3. Set up a wormery or ant colony and record activity over a few weeks.

4. Grow a bean or pea and keep a record of its growth.

5. Grow a bean or pea. When the root and shoot are visible investigate what happens when the seed is turned upside-down and left to continue growing.

6. Collect seeds from various plants and discover how these are protected and dispersed.

7. Investigate what happens to your pulse rate before and after exercise.

Note: Other experiments of comparable standard are acceptable if agreed with the examiner beforehand.

Sportsman

1. Have a broad knowledge of two sports such as Rugby Football, Association Football, Cricket, Hockey, Rounders, Horse Riding, Judo, Archery.

2. Show reasonable proficiency and be taking an active part regularly in at least one of these.

3. Show that you know how to look after the equipment and clothing necessary for the game selected to pass part 2: e.g. blow up a football and take care of your football boots, take care of your cricket bat and know how to look after cricket pads.

4. Show a good sportsmanlike spirit in all Cub Scout games and activities.

5. Know the importance of taking a shower or bath after games if possible, or at least changing out of the clothes worn during the game. Know also the importance of good care of the feet.

Note: Certificates must be produced for part 2 from the Cub Scout Leader or a school teacher and for part 4 from the Cub Scout Leader.

Swimmer

A THREE STAGE BADGE

Stage 1

Perform the following:

1. A jump or dive from the side of the bath.

2. Breathing exercise.

3. Front glide.

4. Back glide.

5. Front paddle 10 metres.

6. Back paddle 10 metres.

7. Backstroke, without the use of arms, hands on hips, 10 metres.

8. 25 metres of either breast-stroke, front crawl or back crawl.

Note: A Cub Scout who holds the Swimming Teachers' Association "Junior Swimmer Badge" qualifies automatically for a Stage 1 Swimmer Badge.

Stage 2

Requirements 1 to 4 to be performed in shirt and shorts or pyjamas.

Perform the following:

1. Tread water for 1 minute in a vertical position.

2. A surface dive to touch the bottom with both hands in at least shoulder depth water.

3. Mushroom float for 5 seconds.

4. Swim across the width of the bath on any front stroke. At the halfway mark turn over on to the back and finish the distance on any back stroke of your choice.

5. Remove clothing whilst in the water, without touching the bottom or side of the bath.

6. Plunge (dive and glide) as far as possible.

7. Commencing with the appropriate racing start, swim 25 metres front or back crawl.

8. Commencing with the appropriate racing start, swim 25 metres breast or butterfly stroke.

Note: A Cub Scout who holds the Swimming Teachers' Association "Cadet Badge" qualifies automatically for a Stage 2 Swimmer Badge.

Stage 3

Perform the following, in the order set out, without a break:

1. Dressed in trousers and shirt or pyjamas, effect an entry from the side of the bath by a straddle or a tuck jump.

2. Swim 45 metres.

3. Tread water for 3 minutes in a vertical position.

4. Undress in the water.

5. Swim 400 metres, surface diving once during the swim, and swimming at least 5 metres completely submerged.

6. Climb out from deep water without the use of steps or assistance.

Note: A Cub Scout who holds the Amateur Swimming Association "Personal Survival" Bronze Award qualifies automatically for a Stage 3 Swimmer Badge.

World Conservation

Carry out these projects as a member of a group of boys and not by yourself. This group could be from your Pack or Six.

1. Take part as a group in two projects, such as:

(a) clearing a ditch, pond or creek;

(b) making, setting up and maintaining a bird feeder, bird table, bird nesting box or bird bath;
(c) creating, cultivating and maintaining a garden and a compost heap;
(d) a nature survey;
(e) an anti-litter campaign;
(f) planting a buddleia bush and keeping a record of the "visitors" to it;
(g) making a footpath map of an area from your own investigation.

Note: Other projects may be undertaken as agreed by the Cub Scout Leader.

2. Go on an expedition with your group into the countryside and:
(a) find some examples showing how man has damaged nature and other examples showing how man has improved nature;
(b) know the *Country Code,* know the reasons for the *Country Code,* and show that you are doing your best to keep it.

3. Carry out the following:
(a) find out all you can about an animal, bird, plant, fish, etc., which is in danger of extinction in your own country; find out what can be done to save it and, if possible, help to do so with expert advice;
(b) find out which creatures and plants are in the greatest danger of extinction in the world and what can be done to save them; find out if you can personally do anything to help save them;
(c) do what you can to inform other people by, for example:
(i) making posters or a display;
(ii) talking to adults (e.g. at a Parents' Evening);
(iii) talking to other young people.

4. With your group find out about one

of the processes of nature, for example:

(a) observe either how a plant grows, a butterfly or frog develops, or some similar process of nature; report on your observations, either using a wall chart, log book, photographs or drawings;

(b) visit a zoo or natural history museum, and make a scrapbook about the feeding habits of one of the animals or birds;

(c) carry out an experiment which shows the effects of pollution in water or in the air and make a chart or display of your findings;

(d) observe and record the effect of the processes of nature in action on a stretch of coastline.

Note: Other projects may be undertaken as agreed by the Cub Scout Leader.

5. Improve your environment by:

(a) planting a tree or shrub;

(b) grassing an area where there is no vegetation cover;

or:

(c) growing plants in a window box or indoors.

Note: Where Cub Scouts are encouraged to carry out a project anywhere near water, for example clearing a ditch or pond or carrying out a small fish survey, leaders must make adequate arrangements for the safety of the Cub Scouts and ensure that the activity is properly supervised.

Bronze

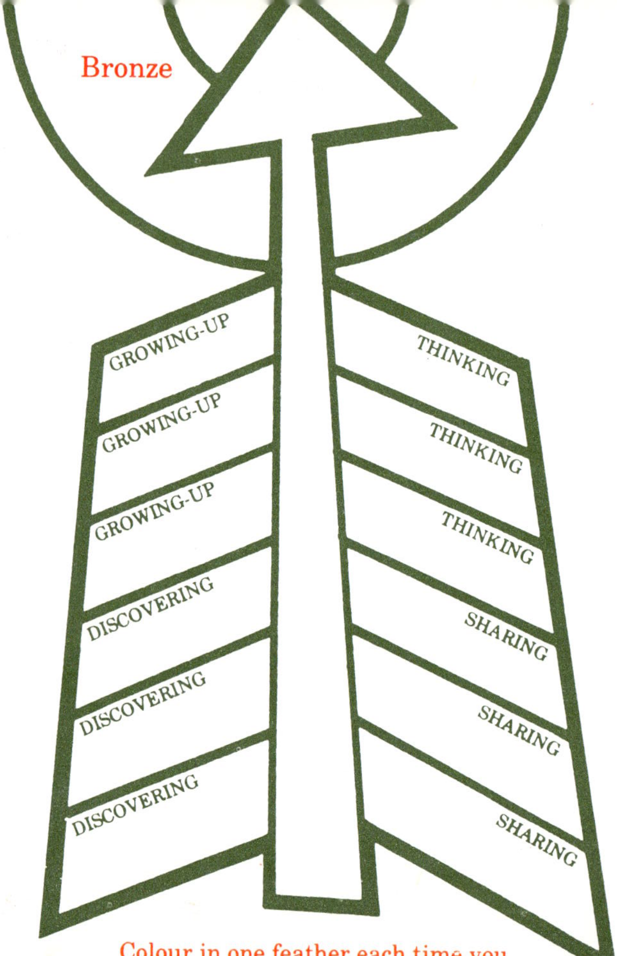

Colour in one feather each time you take part in an activity.

Silver

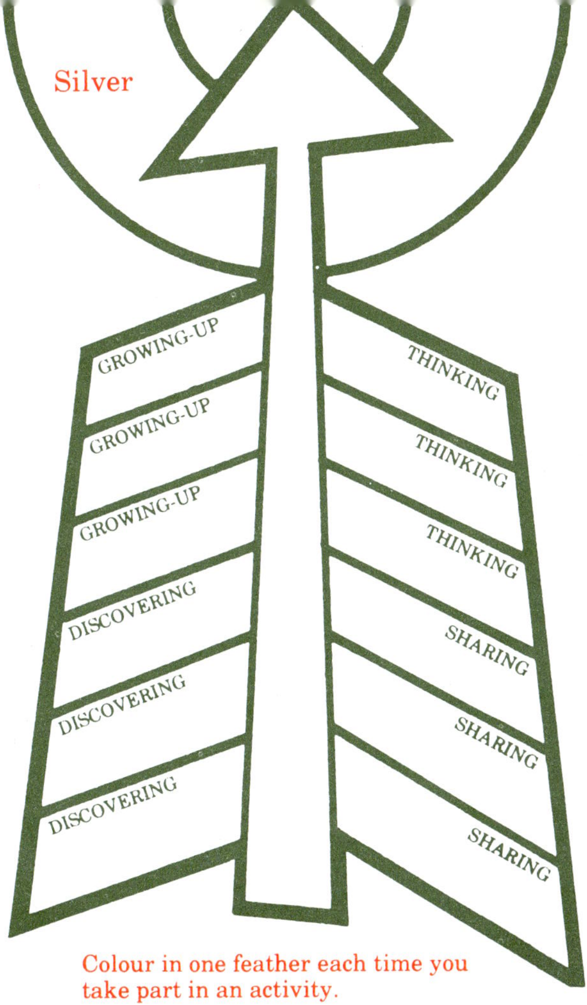

Colour in one feather each time you take part in an activity.

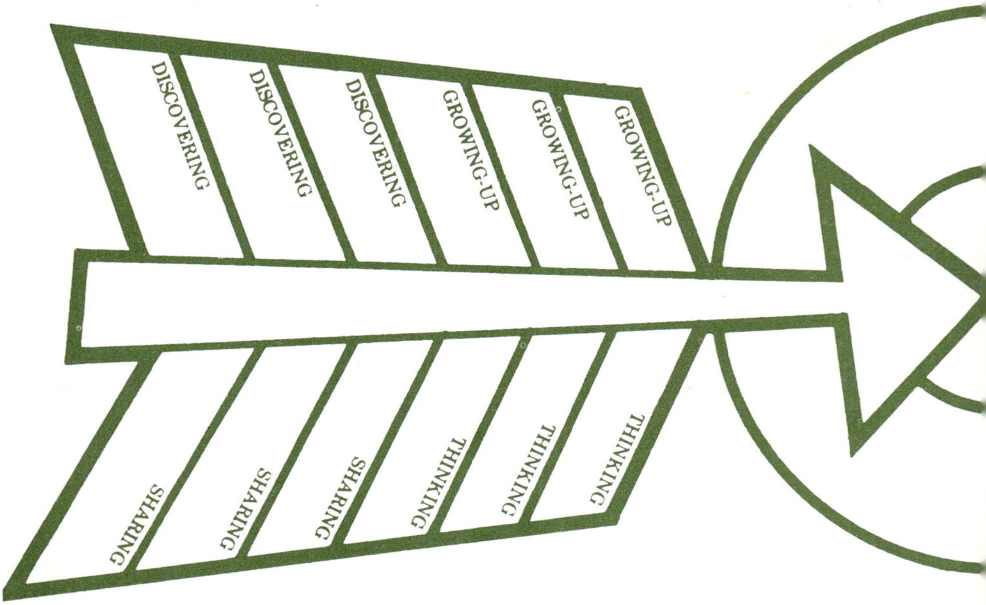
DISCOVERING
DISCOVERING
DISCOVERING
GROWING-UP
GROWING-UP
GROWING-UP
SHARING
SHARING
SHARING
THINKING
THINKING
THINKING

The Link Badge

The Link Badge will help you to get to know all about the Scouts, ready for the time when you join the Troop.

Here is what you do . . .

1. Be at least ten and a half years old.
2. Visit your Scout Leader and register for entry into the Troop before going up.
3. Take part in a Patrol activity out of doors.
4. Show general knowledge of the Scout Movement and the development of world-wide Scouting.
5. Know the Scout Promise and Law and discuss their meaning with your future Scout Leader.

When you are older

Scouts

You will probably already have seen Scouts in your area. They are the next Section of the Movement and are between the ages of 11 and 16. They meet as a Troop and there may be one that meets at your Headquarters or in a hall near where you live. A Troop is made up of a number of Patrols and these, like your Sixes, do all sorts of exciting activities. Patrols are named after animals and birds and will be made up of 6 to 8 Scouts.

As soon as you have gained your Link Badge (see page 61) you can be invested into the Troop. Your Patrol Leader will help you to gain your Scout Standard and Advanced Scout Standard Badges and as you get older you will work for your Chief Scout's Award – but you have to do this on your own.

Venture Scouts

When a Scout leaves the Troop at the age of 16 he will very often join a Venture Scout Unit. This is the last of the training Sections. You will very often find that girls are also Members of a Unit. Not all Scout Groups have a Venture Scout Unit – has your Group got one? Do any Venture Scouts help Akela at Pack Meetings? If your Group does not have a Unit there might be one in your District, ask Akela about it and find out where they meet.

Moving Home?

If you are moving home, perhaps across town or even to another town, which will mean that you cannot attend the same Pack, you will want to join a Pack in your new area as quickly as possible. Finding the Pack nearest to your new home may be difficult and mean that you miss a few week's Meetings but by completing the other side of this page and sending it to the address below you will be a member of a Cub Scout Pack and making lots of new friends even before you have settled down.

Fill in the details on the other side of this page, show it to your Cub Scout Leader or parents, cut the page out and send it to:

The Scout Association,
Records Office,
Churchill Industrial Estate,
LANCING,
West Sussex BN15 8UG

THE SCOUT ASSOCIATION
Records Office
Churchill Industrial Estate
LANCING
West Sussex BN15 8UG

TRANSFER

Name .... Age ....

Present address .... Religion ....

....

at present a member of the ....Pack

is moving to *(full postal address)* ....

....

on ....and wishes to join the nearest suitable Group.
If you are going to live abroad please state if you will be travelling by sea or air.